But along the way did your heart hear us say

That you don't have to earn our love?

...uld do could make us stop loving you

Just the joy that you've brought is enough.

There isn't a thing that the future could bring

That could take back the gift that you are.

a treasure we never could measure.

Just some things we must tell the children.

Janelle and Jeff

PRESENTED TO

Dona and John

FROM

Christmas, '02

DATE

Our love to you and
your special little one

Remember Just WHOSE Child You Are

God Has a Plan You Must Understand

Never Stop Dreaming

Stand Tall Walk Straight

God Has a Plan You Must Understand

You Are a Treasure We Never Could Measure

THINGS
I Must Tell the
CHILDREN

Gloria Gaither

J COUNTRYMAN

Published by J. Countryman®
a division of Thomas Nelson, Inc., Nashville, Tennessee 37214

Designed by Koechel Peterson & Associates, Minneapolis, Minnesota

ISBN 0-8499-5386-8

Printed and bound in Belgium

My parents...

...taught me to be honest regardless of the consequences.

...taught me to be fair even to people I didn't necessarily like.

...taught me to delight and find eternity in the moment.

...taught me balance (i.e. between head and heart, artistic and rational, work and play).

...gave me a sense of humor.

...taught me to turn to Jesus.

...taught me to have confidence in myself.

...taught me to be a cross-generational, cross-cultural friend.

...taught me to know Jesus instead of rules or cultural norms.

...taught me to value work.

...taught me to go against the grain.

...taught me how to make light of success and failure.

...taught me that everything in nature has a name and a purpose.

...taught me to focus on the good in people.

...taught me to have varied interests.

...taught me the joy of learning.

...taught me the importance of good friends.

...taught me to love music and poetry.

...taught me the importance of "hashing it out."

...taught me the unimportance of material things.

...gave me a broad world view.

...told me to search for the truth.

...taught me that there was no limit to what I could do.

...taught me to find a mate who loves God and challenges me.

by Suzanne Gaither Jennings

INTRODUCTION

Most responsible adults take time to make a will and to leave it in a safety deposit box where it will be claimed upon the event of his or her death and dutifully read by some trustee of the estate to the surviving beneficiaries named in that document.

But most of the time the really important things never get mentioned in the will. And most people never get around to saying, let alone writing down, the things they most hope to leave their children...and their children's children.

Yet, whether they get recorded or not, we do pass on to our children the things we value most. And these things are recorded, not so much in our documents as in our days. And the children read the values lived out. They do receive those things valued by their parents, and almost always make them part of their lives.

If our children could unroll and read the "Last Will and Testament" of our lives—if they could watch the documentary of our days on "the big screen," what would they say were the important messages? What would we leave our children to equip them for life in a world so fast-paced that in many ways it does not yet exist?

What if each of us adults—parents or not—were to write our *intangible* LAST WILL AND TESTAMENT. Besides property and tangibles, what would we most like to leave the next generation to equip it for living life?

Over a season of speaking engagements to all parts of the country, I asked of audiences made up of a wide variety of vocations, ages, and backgrounds this question: "If you were to die tomorrow, what would you want to have gotten said to your children to equip them for life—no matter the ages of your children?"

The responses I received amazed and delighted me and for the most part gave me hope. Some made me laugh; others made me cry. Many surprised me and some drove me to my own knees. But let me let you hear from these parents for yourself. Many of these principles—threads and cords for the next generation's moral fabric—echo the ancient scriptures and the documents of our best attempts at governing ourselves. Some are refinements of two millennia of living since the greatest Teacher of all walked the sandy seashores in man-made sandals.

Mostly, these responses are full of hope and joy and, yes, peace. They are, indeed, Some Things We Must Tell the Children.

All the talking

Maturity

and teaching that

has little

parents can do

to do

cannot substitute for

with age.

an actual experience.

FAILURE

IS NOT

TERMINAL.

How can we tell you the things we must tell you

If you want more, take

care of what you have.

Let God do the blessing

instead of your *Ask*

your

doing the taking. *grandparents!*

The things that we want you to know—

Men and women
are different,
always have been,
always will be.

In a world
of dysfunction
only Jesus can
bring function.

only
Jesus

All about living and reasons for giving

Women

of today

can "have it all"—

husband, children,

career, friends—but

there is a price to

pay and it isn't cheap.

Beauty

comes

from

within

Physical beauty is desirable
and can make life easier in
some ways, but it is also fleeting.
DON'T DEPEND ON IT!
Beauty comes from within,
and its symptoms are:
kindness, compassion,
gentleness, joy,
peace, godliness,
patience, contentment.

And things that will help you grow?

Enjoy nature.

Enjoy nature. Never settle for anything less than seeing the earth restored to its original state. God's kingdom is supposed to come on earth, too. Earth is a blessing, and we're supposed to care for our blessings.

Because there is sin in the world, good and righteous people sometimes suffer in ways that seem unjust. Rain falls on both the good and the bad. But in everything, God is "crowding us" into a relationship with Him.

LEARN TO MAKE AT LEAST THREE RECIPES THAT
WERE PASSED ON TO YOUR MOTHER OR FATHER.
KNOW WHO AND WHERE THEY CAME FROM.

No matter how upset you are

with one another in the family,

don't go to bed angry. Agree to say,

"I love you," before you go to sleep.

Oh, we've watched your diet, taught you to be quiet

"Missions"

"Missions" only means caring about people. Give "cups of cold water," anywhere and anytime in the name of Jesus, starting at home with one another.

CAREFULLY CHOOSE MEANINGFUL

NAMES FOR YOUR CHILDREN.

REMIND THEM OFTEN OF

WHAT THEIR NAMES MEAN.

In places of worship and school

Don't live in the past. Marvel in the glory of today: the sunset, the spring flowers, the beauty of small things.

BE CREATIVE AND INNOVATIVE. LOOK FOR MORE THAN ONE WAY TO ACCOMPLISH A TASK.

the beauty of

small things

Read and memorize a proverb a day.

We've kept you well groomed with a nice, tidy room.

HAVE A PERSONAL RELATIONSHIP
WITH GOD. DON'T REST
UNTIL THAT
RELATIONSHIP IS
INTIMATE AND VITAL.

Celebrate your
spiritual birthday!

And we've mentioned the Golden Rule.

Prime

Tuck your children in at night
(no matter what age).
This is prime heart time.

HONOR YOUR MATE.

THE JOY OF SERVANTHOOD

heart

STARTS WITH YOUR MOST PRIMARY RELATIONSHIP.

time

Be as sincerely sorry over breaking a promise
as over breaking a treasured possession.

But along the way did your heart hear us say

LEAVE THE ONES YOU LOVE

"REFRIGERATOR MESSAGES."

Treasure

Treasure family

stories of great

family

experiences. Write

Read a Bible
story every night
before sleep, even
when you're grown-up.

them down,

stories

pass them on.

That you don't have to earn our love?

Stay in church.

The church isn't perfect,

but like the ark,

it's the best ship afloat!

Remember that
God has no
grandchildren,
only children.
Know Him
for yourself.

Not a thing you could do could make us stop loving you

Morality, integrity, and respect for the rights of others must be based on the principles of God's Word. We can't just make up "standards of conduct." There must be a yardstick to measure our behavior, and God's love is the only truly trustworthy standard of conduct.

Morality

Integrity

Respect

THE EASY THING IS NOT ALWAYS THE RIGHT THING. SOMETIMES THE RIGHT THING IS VERY HARD, BUT ALWAYS DO THE RIGHT THING.

Just the joy that you've brought is enough.

God is involved in your life.

Seek His direction on everything,

even the small stuff.

care for

God wants us to care for His earth.
Love nature. Preserve, replant, and respect
other living things and defend their intended
place in the environment. Notice, enjoy,
and treasure the details of God's work.

His earth

Remember:

Remember: Things are dispensable; people are not.

Never treasure things more than people.

There isn't a thing that the future could bring

Know Jesus for yourself and turn to Him for everything. Worship God alone—not religious cultural trappings—and align everything else to this central priority.

Really care about others and try to see where they are coming from. Protect their feelings and personhood. Never look down on anyone else, but raise others who are down by loving and respecting them.

GIVE YOURSELF AWAY FOR THE THINGS THAT LAST FOREVER. DON'T BE CAREFUL ABOUT SAVING YOURSELF WHEN OTHERS ARE IN NEED.

Love and treasure God's Word and read it daily with a sincere heart to discover the character and intent of God.

Don't be impressed or influenced by superficial standards of beauty, success, popularity, or status. Learn to see, recognize, and value real character and to treasure the simplest gift given from a sincere heart.

GRANDPARENTS ARE THE KEEPERS OF A CHILD'S CREDENTIALS.

That could take back the gift that you are.

Throw your hat in the air!

Jump into a pile of leaves!

Blow up some balloons!

Build a good bonfire!

Make a snowman!

Pick some apples!

Dive in!

Celebrate all of life.

Celebrate all of life

Be big enough to admit when you are wrong. Say I'm sorry. Resolve a conflict. Make amends. No price is too high for a clear conscience.

When you have kids, work together
and make work a joy. Rake leaves
(and jump in them). Plant
a garden (and eat the vegetables).
Shovel the snow (and build a snow fort).
Build a grape arbor, plant grapes
(and make grape jelly). Pick up the
sticks in the yard (and have a wiener roast).

You are a treasure we never could measure.

Start and end the day with a prayer.

Persevere. Don't give up on yourself, your friends, your children, your parents, your marriage, or your circumstances.

LEARN TO FORGIVE OTHERS.

THAT WAY YOU'LL BE ABLE TO FORGIVE YOURSELF.

Learn to Forgive others

To be loved is a treasure, to love is priceless.

Believe in people,

but trust the Lord.

Just some things we must tell the children.

God's law was meant to protect and free us, not to confine us. There is freedom in the safe boundaries of God's law.

The smallest good deed is grander than the best of intentions.

I'm sure we've told you to mind all your manners.

YOUR VOICE COUNTS!

—You can always call home.

—You can always leave the party.

—You can always use us (your parents) for an excuse.

—You can always say no.

—You can always do the right thing.

—You are never alone.

You are never alone.

Treasure your family and love your siblings. No wonder Jesus said to His children, "I will know if you love me by the way you love one another."

Always deal justly, but remember that things aren't always fair here in this life. Live with an eternal perspective.

And to get to appointments on time.

Some Things I Must Tell the Children

How can we tell you the things we must tell you,
The things that we want you to know—
All about living and reasons for giving,
And things that will help you grow?
Oh, we've watched your diet, taught you to be quiet
In places of worship and school,
We've kept you well groomed with a nice, tidy room,
And we've mentioned the Golden Rule.
But along the way did your heart hear us say
That you don't have to earn our love?
Not a thing you could do could make us stop loving you—
Just the joy that you've brought is enough.
There isn't a thing that the future could bring
That could take back the gift that you are;
You are a treasure we never could measure.
Just some things we must tell the children.

I'm sure we've told you to mind all your manners,
And to get to appointments on time,
And we remind you to hang up your clothes,
And finish the homework assigned.
And you've learned to care for your teeth and your hair,
And you make your own bed everyday;
You got decent grades and your lunch money's paid,
And you won your first game yesterday.
But did we make it clear, were you able to hear,
As you skipped through the house and our lives
That God has a plan that you must understand
No matter how much you "arrive."
Never stop dreaming, keep working and singing,
But remember just Whose child you are,
Stand tall and walk straight, and be home before eight.
Just some things we must tell the children.
And whatever you do, remember: we love you.
Just some things we must tell the children.

Words by Gloria Gaither Music by William J. Gaither ©1980-81 by William J. Gaither (ASCAP)

Communication

and understanding

in any relationship

are worth the struggle.

Don't take the easy

way out and die inside.

There is a difference

between what is

essential and what

is incidental. Only

one of these is

worth fighting for.

And we remind you to hang up your clothes.

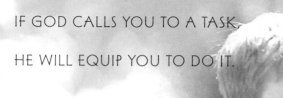

IF GOD CALLS YOU TO A TASK,

HE WILL EQUIP YOU TO DO IT.

Integrity and character is the
most timeless legacy you
can leave behind.

Be as gentle and
understanding to others
as you wish they would be to you.

*Integrity
and
character*

And finish the homework assigned.

When you visit a distressed country or area of your own country, pack or wear extra clothes so you can leave some with those in need.

Think about the good things—

in people, in life, in the world, in yourself. Live with a

YES in your attitude.

Live with a yes in your attitude

Realize that there is no limit

to what you can do, even

"More is caught than taught"
is a principle of life.
By living out what
you believe, others
will know who you
are and what
you stand for.

with limitations.

You've learned to care for your teeth and your hair.

Angels are real.

Satan is real.

Germs are real.

The wind is real.

God is real.

And you make your own bed everyday!

Life is meant to be enjoyed. Work hard. Play hard. Sleep soundly. Laugh a lot. Cry when you hurt. Pick and smell the flowers. Hug every day. Take deep breaths. "Sing, sing, sing your hearts out to God!" (Col. 3:16, The Message)

Learn contentment. See the treasure of this moment, of what you have and are now. The only way God can trust His children with more is if they take care of what they already have.

Learn contentment

Appreciate the value, necessity, and joy of a good friend!

Gratitude seems to be our most fulfilling response to God. When you don't know what to say to God, say "Thanks."

Life is a journey in pursuit of God.

Following Him is the great adventure.

LEARN TO LISTEN. IN LISTENING TO GOD,

WE GAIN WISDOM. IN LISTENING TO OURSELVES,

WE LEARN INSIGHT. IN LISTENING TO OTHERS,

WE LEARN COMPASSION.

You got decent grades and your lunch money's paid.

Don't worry about your enemies. They will leave you alone and probably ignore you. But choose your friends carefully, for they have the greatest potential to influence you.

Choose your friends carefully

Work together as a family. Before you begin each job, choose one family member to read or tell stories as the others work. This will bring the family together, not only by tasks accomplished together, but by a huge body of great literature shared. It will also teach your children to value the "story keepers" of our world as much as those who produce products.

And you won your first game yesterday.

Work on your communication skills. Begin

by listening as if you really care about

what the other person is expressing.

Not everyone can be a great singer.

Not everyone can be a good chess player. But

everyone can improve the ability to communicate.

Work continuously on communications.
Almost all family problems—
or problems in any kind of
relationship—can be
avoided or solved
with good communication.

The gift of choice is one of God's greatest gifts. We always have it with us. Sometimes our power to choose is obvious, sometimes it is subtle. But it is always there.

There are always consequences to our motives, behaviors, attitudes. These may be positive, life-giving, energizing, freeing. They may be negative, destructive, life-sapping, binding. Seldom are they neutral.

But did we make it clear, were you able to hear.

You have two ways to sing your life's song: Do-Be, Do-Be, Do-Be

OR

Be-Do, Be-Do, Be-Do

Remember what you are is more important than what you do.

As you skipped through the house and our lives

Don't be afraid to confront and challenge others,

but make sure your honest confrontation is

motivated by a genuine concern for their

well-being and a desire to encourage

them on their journey to

becoming more like God.

WE ARE ALL SERVANTS

TO SOMETHING OR SOMEONE.

CHOOSE YOUR MASTER CAREFULLY.

Embrace life

Embrace life—all of it. Do not run from pain, struggle, crisis, or grief, but recognize these as the tools for carving out places in your soul for joy, love, reconciliation, peace, and contentment.

Laugh...a lot!

Belly laughs cleanse the spirit. All kinds of laughter are good— smile, giggle, snicker, chuckle, crack up! Don't forget to laugh at yourself, always forget to laugh at others. Life is funny. God made a wild and amusing assortment of creatures and plants. He must have a great sense of humor!

Explore. Ask questions, take trips, read a wide variety of great books. Every field of learning is interesting if you begin to explore it.

Notice the wonders everywhere.

angels like to visit

Treasure your home. Make it sweet to see, hear, smell, taste, feel. Sharing your home with others is one of life's great joys. Even angels like to visit other people's homes!

other people's homes!

KNOW HOW TO RECOGNIZE, APPRECIATE,

AND CELEBRATE A "MAGICAL MOMENT."

That God has a plan that you must understand

Develop the fine art of trustworthiness. Be "known" for having a good sense of responsibility so that others consider your word dependable and your actions consistent with your word. Follow through, even when no one would ever know.

Love beauty. See that life is filled

with good music, great literature, the

wonder of nature, and the joy of creativity.

Have an appreciation for the creativity

of others—and, most of all, of God!

No matter how much you "arrive".

Take care of your body. Eat whole foods, avoid chemicals, and exercise outside as much as you can by doing real activities like walking to work or school, climbing hills, hiking trails, swimming, rowing a boat, working at manual jobs. Sleep like a baby. Get up early. Keep a regular schedule. Be a regular person. Fill your mind with good things.

Have a healthy self-concept without being self-centered.

GOOD MANNERS ARE SIMPLY CARING FOR OTHERS AND THINKING OF THEIR NEEDS AND FEELINGS.

Let the important topics of the spirit have
a natural and comfortable place in your
everyday conversation—at the table, at
your work, in your relationships. If there
is no friend like Jesus, His name
should come up quite often.

YOU ARE TEACHING YOUR CHILDREN HOW TO TREAT

THEIR PARENTS BY THE WAY YOU'RE TREATING YOURS.

Choose a marriage partner who has
his/her own close relationship with God.
As you love each other more, seek
God daily. As you grow toward the
Lord, you will grow closer to each other.
"A house divided against itself cannot stand."

There are special places in the world that restore the

soul, quiet places where you can be alone with

God—the woods, the seashore, the desert, the

prairie, the lakeside, the riverbank. Find

your place and go there often.

Jesus did.

Never stop dreaming, keep working and singing.

When you're dizzy with activities, crazy with stress, stand still and look up. God is there. Talk and listen to Him. He speaks to you in His Word. Be still and know....

GOD KNOWS WE NEED TO BE IN HIM TO BE COMPLETE. HE DOESN'T SHARE OUR ALLEGIANCE. SERVING OTHER MASTERS WILL DESTROY US. KEEP GOD IN THE CENTER.

Save sexual intercourse for marriage. Don't have sexual relationships outside of marriage. This act brings two people together in a way that is like no other, and it is especially sacred because it can produce an eternal soul. Everything about this act is protected and guarded by God's laws: Thou shalt not commit adultery.

there

But remember just Whose child you are,

Treasure the positive, good friends in your life. A true friend is a gift more valuable than possessions.

Don't try to create your own God, or make up a God according to your own definition. God is. His Word tells us about Him. Read it daily to get to know more and more about His ways and attributes.

DON'T THROW AROUND

OR DESECRATE GOD'S NAME.

Keep God's special day holy. Don't use it for your own affairs—don't work to make money on this day. God gave us six out of seven days for our use. Keep one day for rest and for enriching your relationships with Him and His family.

Don't take life

into your own hands

—not someone else's

—not your own.

Don't kill.

Don't lie about another person. Don't tell something that is not true about anyone.

Don't let your heart become a thief. Don't wish you had someone else's stuff, someone else's wife or husband, someone else's status or circumstances, or someone else's life history. Where you let your heart go, your actions are sure soon to follow.

If you experience hard times because you choose to do the right thing, you can be confident in asking God to take care of you. He will; He promised.

(I HAVE NEVER SEEN THE RIGHTEOUS FORSAKEN OR THEIR CHILDREN BEGGING FOR BREAD. PSALM 77:25)

Stand tall and walk straight, and be home before eight.

Let Jesus be your best friend. This friendship will teach you how to make and keep other friendships and what to treasure in those relationships.

LIVING FOR GOD IS ONLY HARD IF YOU HALF-LIVE IT.

The only way to avoid criticism is to say nothing, do nothing, be nothing. Live to please God, not the critics.

Just some things we must tell the children.

Treasure your relationships with your siblings. Work to resolve any conflicts; reconcile any differences. God intended for siblings to dwell together in unity.

Your family will spend a lot of time in the car. Make it God-time. Sing songs, listen to tapes, play games, read to one another, tell Bible stories, share what God is doing in your lives.

LOVE PEACE. MAKE PEACE. ENJOY PEACE. PRAY FOR PEACE. BRING PEACE.

Choose carefully. Every choice has consequences. Accept the consequences of your choices. Celebrate the good ones, learn from the bad ones.

Get into the habit of hospitality. Include single mothers and their children, widows, someone far from their own family. Invite someone home for dinner or to join your family on an outing. Even Jesus had a cookout for His friends.

Do the next thing

God's will for

your life is

do the next thing

You can never do anything to make me or God stop loving you.

Forget when people "do you bad." Remember when they "do you good."

YOU CAN DO NOTHING TO MAKE GOD LOVE YOU MORE.

And whatever you do, remember, we love you.

ALWAYS LET YOUR HEART BE
BROKEN BY THE THINGS THAT
BREAK THE HEART OF GOD.

It is okay to try
and fail. It is not
okay to refuse to try.
Never say "I can't." If
something needs to be done,
there is always a way to do it.

Learning is a
lifelong joy and
adventure. Be
a student. As
long as you
learn, you live.
The more you
learn, the more
you will discover
you have yet
to learn.

We often grow through our failures, but success can be a killer. Keep both successes and failures in perspective.

WHEN YOU START A TASK, DO IT WELL, DO IT RIGHT, AND DO IT ALL.

Never settle into your comfort zone. Let God keep pushing you into new territory.

Just some things we must tell the children.

I'm sure we've told you to mind all your manners,

And to get to appointments on time,

And we remind you to hang up your clothes,

Never stop d...

And finish the homework assigned...

You've learned to care for your teeth and your hair.

And you make your own...

And you won your first game yesterday.

You got decent grades and your lunch money,

But did we make it clear, were you...